Household debt assistance the Dutch way

Household debt assistance, the Dutch way

Essay, non-fiction, independently published.

Amazon paperback edition, 5.5" x 8.5", glossy cover.

Printed in color on premium white paper in Britannic Bold and Bookman Old Style.

ISBN: 9798324065881

Cover photo: Walid Ahmad (via Pexels)

Version date: 27 June 2025

Keywords: poverty, inequality, household debt, municipalities, government policies, landlords, utility companies

Notes

You can contact me via angelinasouren@gmail.com. Keep in mind that my emails do not always reach me, so you may have to try a few times or try to contact me via a different communication channel.

Household debt assistance the Dutch way

Angelina Souren

Table of contents

Foreword

"In many, many cases, the most effective way of helping people in extreme poverty is simply to give them unconditional cash in a single lump sum transfer and get out the way," said Rory Stewart in an interview in September 2024. Stewart is a former Member of Parliament and government minister for the UK's Conservative Party. In 2019, he left the Conservatives. He was mostly referring to his experience in international development, but what he said also holds true for poverty in the developed world.

On 28 February 2024, the Netherlands' *Nationale Ombudsman* issued the rapport "Hoe eerder hoe beter" (the sooner, the better). It addresses a process called "vroegsignalering" (early alerts, early detection), which concerns informing the local municipality of arrears and actions that can then be taken by the local municipality. It's the creditors who report the arrears, not the debtors. It's also staff at the local municipalities as well as staff at companies and organizations that municipalities have agreements with who report citizens for *vroegsignalering*.

- The Ombudsman concluded that the way this *vroegsignalering* process works is still far from ideal.

- Reportedly, the IMF recently stated that there currently is no best practice for household debt assistance.

Having lived in England for around two decades and having seen first-hand what massive inequality looks like, I was horrified when I stumbled upon *vroegsignalering*. The Netherlands has definitely become more polarized. It's hard to see how a democratic western government not only can be comfortable with this system of *vroegsignalering*, but has plans to expand it and start including study loans.

I believe that *vroegsignalering* can increase inequality and take agency away from perfectly capable people. The reasoning behind *vroegsignalering* appears to be judgmental. It tends to otherize people who have debts and assign blame to them, discount their opinions and experiences and label them as lacking in skills and insights instead of simply having less money coming in than needs to go out each month.

This is a hallmark of inequality, the fact that the opinions, interests and experiences of some groups in society are invalidated.

The photo on the next page shows a scene in England, which has far greater inequality than the Netherlands. Prosperous smaller property owners as well as property developers feel free to dump their rubbish where low-income tenants are living. Such tenants' wishes and needs don't matter much. Their opinions and experiences are too easily – often habitually – dismissed in societies with great inequality.

Developers often buy up old, small homes and build small, cheap housing to rent out, with as goal to tear it all down eventually. They have no interest in looking after these properties because they need to be able to get permission to demolish it all in the future. It is in their interest to allow these properties to become derelict or develop problems such as massive rubbish dumping. Rubbish usually constitutes a fire hazard, but rubbish affects the tenants of these properties, not their owners.

Is this what we want to see happening in the Netherlands too?

Traditional debt advice – which is just another money-making industry with no altruistic thoughts at its base – can actually plunge people into major financial problems that they didn't have before. I believe that *vroegsignalering* runs the same risk of causing problems for people instead of helping them. That's for example because of the extensive and expanding data sharing that is tied to it. It can end up blocking access for people instead of opening doors and clearing roadblocks for them. *Vroegsignalering* needs certain municipalities to take the lead and become shining examples, the guides that set the standard for others.

Vroegsignalering is currently far too Orwellian. In England, the phrase "nanny state" is often used with regard to the provision of benefits and advice about healthy eating and so on, but *vroegsignalering* is an indication of what a real nanny state would look like, with a Gattaca-like stratified society.

The Dutch government should regulate much better what creditors can do and must do within the context of *vroegsignalering*. At the moment, the process lacks integrity and primarily serves creditors.

While I have a primary background in earth & life science, I have now spent more than a decade looking into *bioethics sensu lato*, which includes inequality challenges such as poverty and questions about fairness. Any mistakes in this booklet are mine, however.

I decided to dedicate this booklet to my mother, Cherdin Herberighs, who passed away in 1975. I don't believe that she'd ever known true economic hardship though she did experience the Second World War. I think that she too would be taken aback by the idea of *vroegsignalering*. Her mother, my grandmother, would certainly have a lot to say about random strangers invading people's homes to look into their finances because they are behind on a few bills. I've read that there is talk about even including internet access and phone bills in *vroegsignalering* because arrears of a mere tenner can get people cut off. It would be far better to get the phone providers to stop slapping on high late-payment fines.

Vroegsignalering runs the risk of stopping people from running their own lives, making their own, effective decisions and setting their own priorities. It can be immensely judgmental and the judgment, sometimes leading to actions being taken, can be based on nothing else but mere assumptions and, astonishingly, zero actual information.

In his well-known TED Talk, Rutger Bregman pointed out that poverty is the result of a lack of cash, not of character. (In 2019, Bregman famously lambasted the World Economic Forum at Davos about the failure to tax the rich.) UN Rapporteur and human rights law professor Olivier de Schutter said, in 2022, that povertyism should be illegal, just like racial discrimination and other forms of discrimination. I concur.

To this I also add that as long as the Dutch process of "schuldhulpverlening" can be shown in advance to have little else but commercial interests at heart, clients should do their best to avoid it. It appears to be largely a punitive or narcissistic and possibly moneymaking exercise in which false reassurances are easily given to get clients to sign up to it but not put in writing. Clients should ask themselves why staff never asks them whether they have enough to eat and whether municipal taxes have been waived, which they are bound to be eligible for if they don't have enough income to cover the basics.

In August 2024, the Dutch Humanitas network started running a petition to stop the debt exploitation processes from which everyone appears to benefit, including the government, except the clients. (I didn't sign it because of the vague manner in which the petition was phrased.)

Latest videos
"Bedrijven én de overheid verdienen geld over de rug van kwetsbare mensen."
Hans, vrijwilliger Humanitas
Teken nu de petitie
Meer informatie

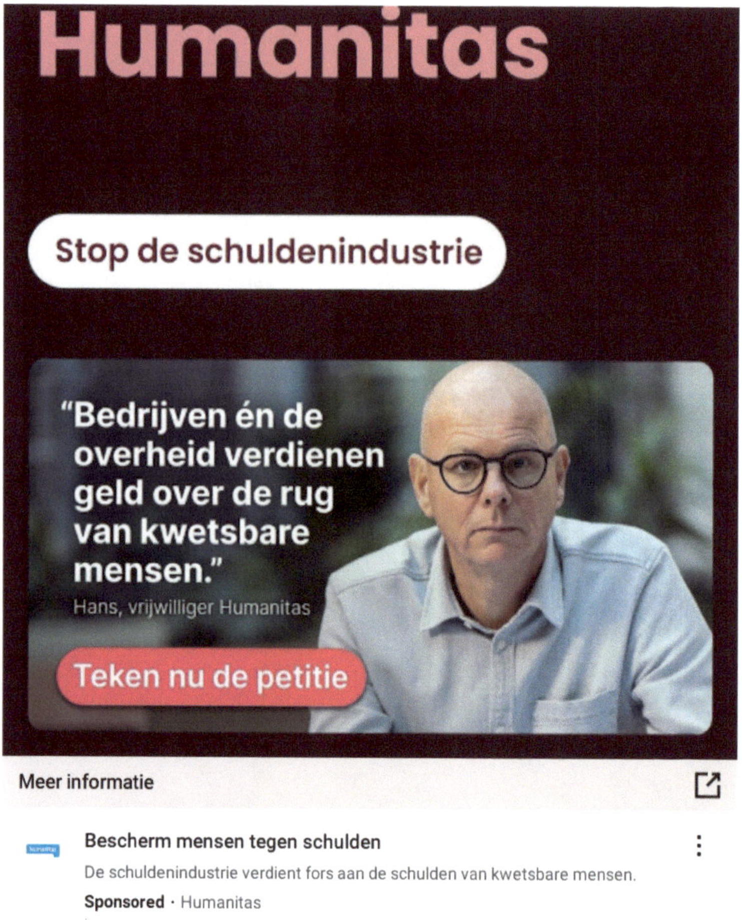

Bescherm mensen tegen schulden

De schuldenindustrie verdient fors aan de schulden van kwetsbare mensen.

Sponsored · Humanitas

1. Fundamentally flawed

According to the 2024 report by the Nationale Ombudsman, around 42% of Dutch households at least occasionally pay a bill late these days. Problem debts, by contrast, can cause a lot of stress and affect people's health. The number of households in the Netherlands with problem debts increased from 618,000 in 2021 to 726,000 in 2023.

While it's true that household debts can both be the result of financial crises and can result in a financial crisis if they spiral out of control, the Dutch *vroegsignalering* process risks alienating many people and causing instead of resolving problems for them, for various reasons.

Making one payment late can already trigger it and start robbing you of your rights just because you are not wealthy.

This early identification of households with arrears through *vroegsignalering* is fundamentally flawed as it is administered and overseen by the largest household debt creditor in the Netherlands. That's the government, including the local municipalities.

As of 1 January 2021, so-called *vastelastenpartners* have a legal obligation within the *Wet gemeentelijke schuldhulpverlening* (*Wgs*) to alert local government about a household's arrears. This concerns fixed expenses such as rent, possibly also water board taxes and income tax debts, local government taxes, energy costs, water bills and health insurance premiums. Internet access or mobile phone costs are not included, but the legislation has room for them.

Online search results reveal that the aim of *vroegsignalering* is not to benefit debtors but 1) to diminish the state's debt assistance expenses and 2) to help shift funds toward creditors. Potential benefits for debtors – such as the prevention or remediation of depression, social isolation and nutritional deprivation – are not often mentioned. There isn't even much attention for the related health expenses.

In a 2021 interview in *Vastgoedmarkt*, the head of one of the country's largest housing providers and real estate enterprises stated that they aim to be like a caring dad for their tenants. That sounds promising. It could be interesting to see how this organization is using its clout to promote a far more positive attitude among housing providers than the housing market is generally known for.

They aren't the first real estate outfit in the world that eagerly wants to change the negative reputation of the real estate industry. It's not easy, but it always appears to start with simply setting a great example for others to follow. (I had an interesting discussion about this on LinkedIn a few years ago with a housing developer in Australia who someone else had tipped me about.)

Foreign readers may need to be told that health insurance is mandatory in the Netherlands. The monthly premium for an adult is currently around EUR 150 and the standard insurance for adults does not include costs for dentistry. The state-mandated reimbursement threshold ("eigen risico") is currently around EUR 400. Costs related to dentistry do count toward the threshold; at least, that is what I read somewhere, but I also read somewhere that at the start of the year, you get paid the threshold amount that you didn't use up in the previous year and that turned out to be incorrect. (It's basically one big administrative mess for which having a Zen attitude comes in handy.)

Certain conditions must have been met before a creditor can report arrears to the local government. That is, the creditor can report the debtor, but if the conditions have not been met, the municipality has to ignore this. It is a major challenge for municipalities to sort through the incoming reports.

Creditors must have tried to resolve the issue directly with the debtor. (This is called "sociale incasso" or social collection, in other words: without involving the courts.) This often does not happen at all.

There is a similarity between British Section 21 Notices (no-fault evictions) and *vroegsignalering*. The latter is often activated much too early, "just in case", for legal reasons, just like Section 21 Notices are often handed to tenants as if they were candy, "just in case", for legal reasons (meeting the time limit). This is a sign that *vroegsignalering* may be increasing inequality instead of ameliorating it.

As all of the involved parties except the debtor but including the local government have a financial interest in the matter, none of them can be neutral. That's the fatal fundamental flaw in this process.

There is a considerable power imbalance in this situation and it's hugely skewed away from the household. Having a power imbalance is enough to cause disadvantages for the party with the least power and can thereby alone already increase inequality. There is no requirement for biases for that to happen.

The fact that all these parties have a financial interest in the household can make it extremely hard for a household to get straight answers, unlike when a debt is discussed in court. Sometimes, the fixed expense parties are so driven by suspicion that they use *vroegsignalering* to go on fishing expeditions.

As result of this, *vroegsignalering* is often activated much too early. When people get pestered when there is no actual problem, it can increase mistrust – or is it distrust – in democracy and in government. That, in turn, can drive people away from seeking support when they should.

All around the western world, not only trust in science and scientists, but also trust in democracy and government is declining. Those are worrisome developments that should be kept at the back of people's minds when sculpting a process that is as eerily Orwellian as *vroegsignalering.*

In a 2023 IMF working paper (WP/23/92) that discusses effects of the European debt crisis (which started in 2009), the authors call household debt distress "an economic rather than a legal problem". Irrespective of whether my interpretation of this is correct or even relevant, I think that it is very important to note this because *vastelastenpartners* see household debt distress as purely a legal issue.

In the same IMF paper, over-indebtedness is defined as a situation in which consumers are no longer able to meet their future financial obligations. The overall deterioration of people's economic situation will then gradually lead to social exclusion, a higher cost of living (as the poor pay more) and a declining level of participation in overall economic development and social progress (which boils down to social exclusion), states this 2023 IMF paper (which refers to a 2003 paper by Reifner et al. here). Note that these – the declining participation in life in general and the increase in household expenses – are results, not causes.

Here we have another major problem within *vroegsignalering*. A frequent assumption appears to be that personal problems (such as mental health issues, addiction or an inability to keep track of expenses or to complete forms) are the cause of a household's problematic financial situation. This assumption can be immensely off-putting and does not inspire trust in government and democracy either.

It remains unclear to me what exactly *vroegsignalering* can do for consumers other than offering to make calls to arrange repayment schedules, which many consumers are perfectly capable of doing themselves. Moreover, what *vroegsignalering* can do is (still) highly dependent on the municipality in question.

2. Transparency, clarity and completeness

There is currently a near-complete lack of transparency. Most households in the Netherlands will never have heard of *vroegsignalering*. Creditors are supposed to inform debtors when they contact local government about arrears, within this *vroegsignalering* context, but it is currently sufficient for a debtor to include in its communications a sentence that states that the debtor may contact the local municipality.

Here we see the power imbalance being expressed again. Why not give the debtor complete, transparent and clear information about this *vroegsignalering* process? This is so that the debtor can be blindsided. There is no good explanation for the lack of information given to the debtor other than that the process seems geared toward disempowering debtors.

Part of the lack of transparency that is the result of the fundamental flaw of *vroegsignalering* is the absence of clarity and completeness. When hardly any information is given to the debtor, it can neither be complete nor clear.

For starters, it must be made very clear what powers the people have who start ringing doorbells, making calls and leaving cards and letters within this *vroegsignalering* process.

At the very least, the term *vroegsignalering* should also be mentioned so that people can at least search for it on the internet.

As long as this is not dealt with in a better way, this duty rests on the shoulders of the creditor who wants to start the process. That is the party who should give the debtor complete, transparent and clear information about the *vroegsignalering* process.

That party should also make clear that the debtor has the right to tell the creditor not to alert the local authorities.

The main goal of the *vroegsignalering* process should not be to ambush the debtor for the sake of enabling the creditor to show a court that the debtor "refused" all assistance and paint the debtor as an uncooperative troublemaker.

If information handed to a debtor states that engagement with *vroegsignalering* is entirely voluntarily and without obligation, then that should stand for something in practice.

In the current situation, particularly the information provided to debtors about *vroegsignalering* is still often geared toward what the municipalities (and the creditors) need, which is to fulfill their obligations under the "Wgs" legislation. The message is often "We don't care about who you are, how you feel about any of this or about what you actually need. We have to do something and you'll have to put up with it. If you don't, we will label to you a troublemaker and that's that."

Creditors can even get away with refusing to give debtors a detailed justification of what debtors owe. They can inflate outstanding amounts too easily, merely to strengthen their claims. Staff at the local municipality involved in *vroegsignalering* obviously can't help with that. Debtors can be given the runaround when parties keep referring to one another as the source to contact and get this information from. When debtors still need to engage lawyers to extract that kind of information, this signals very clearly that *vroegsignalering* is not very effective.

Also needing to be guaranteed is absolute clarity as to who gives what kind of information to whom within this context. When debtors deal with various staff within the *vroegsignalering* process at the local municipality, they don't know who has been given which information. It's currently often clear that some information has been passed on between colleagues but the extent is not clear. This can cause a lot of confusion and uncertainty. It is a potential basis for miscommunications.

How come employee X knows that the debtor has energy bill arrears when the debtor has not told employee X about this? What else has employee X been told and by whom? Debtors should not have to wonder. It should be clear. Otherwise, the client might assume that employee X also knows about the change in a personal situation and then be fined for not having informed the municipality.

3. Cultural differences and privacy concerns

There currently is no uniform approach in *vroegsignalering*. What the local municipalities do depends on how much staff and budget they have available and on who runs which departments as well as on who the big commercial players are that are important for the municipality. It can be a mere exercise of ticking the required boxes often enough.

As a result, there often is no awareness of the fact that information should not only be clear, transparent, complete and available in different languages, but that people from different backgrounds may experience debts very differently, hence deal with them very differently. They may also be highly alarmed by the immense invasion of privacy and erosion of agency that *vroegsignalering* can constitute.

In the United Kingdom, for example, where inequality is much greater than in the Netherlands, people whose behavior is exemplary and who have no arrears can be evicted too, through a so-called Section 21 Notice. For years now, the UK government has been saying that it wishes to abolish these so-called no-fault evictions. It was even part of the Conservatives' 2019 election manifesto. This has remained empty talk. It is an expression of inequality. Well-to-do people don't rent. They don't get served Section 21 Notices. They serve them.

As a result, whereas Dutch people may freak out over the threat of eviction, many Brits and people who have lived in Britain may not at all. This means that particularly Brits living in the Netherlands may not understand what all the fuss is about when people from the municipality start banging on their doors because they paid their water bill or rent late. They might do their utmost to pay their municipal taxes in time, however.

Also owing to the lack of clarity (not just because for example the process is often activated too early, for legal reasons), completeness and transparency in the information handed to the debtors, *vroegsignalering* can quickly become highly counterproductive.

For people who are from countries with highly restrictive regimes, *vroegsignalering* activities may certainly cause a lot of stress and exacerbate the situation rather than resolve it.

The privacy violations committed during the execution of *vroegsignalering* appear to be legal as long as they are committed as part of the municipalities' duties within the legislation (*Wet gemeentelijke schuldhulpverlening* or *Wgs*).

That's a pretty shocking expression of inequality. People's rights are ruthlessly eroded on the mere basis of the fact that they have one or more payment arrears and that their data were not yet included in one or both of the two databases of people with problem debts or were included, but longer than six months ago.

Data are currently kept for six months after which they are anonymized. Is there is such a thing as anonymizing people's debts and personal situations? The data will likely always remain identifiable, also when the debtors and creditors' names, addresses and date of birth have been removed.

This information, too, should be communicated to the debtors. There can be a complete lack of information and transparency in this regard. The debtor has no idea what to count on.

When people knock on debtors' doors and have loud conversations through those doors with complete disregard for neighbors who may be able to hear the conversation in some apartment buildings, then that too is an expression of inequality.

A major component of *vroegsignalering* often appears to be the assumption that personal challenges, such as presumed autism, lead to debts, whereas most debts are purely the result of the fact that people's fixed outgoings are much higher than their income.

If you have little income, you sometimes have to take a risk and shift your priorities temporarily. An example could be that someone decides to pay the rent late because it enables the person to start up a business that will quickly generate enough income. It could also be because the person is self-employed and knows that a good client will soon pay a large invoice but would like to make an investment now rather than in two months when a discount will have run out.

A parent can choose to pay late when an expense for a child takes precedence and the level of income is relatively low but still high enough to be able to make up soon.

It's utterly nuts to send *vroegsignalering* staff over to bang on these people's doors, but this is what currently happens in some municipalities. This may particularly be the case when it concerns for example a real estate outfit with a large number of properties in the municipality.

4. More exciting approaches

The Dutch city of Arnhem is launching a two-year project (spearheaded by city councillor Mark Lauriks, as announced on 23 April 2024) in which the city will actually pay all the debts of its 60 poorest households.

The city council acknowledges that debts can keep people stuck and can rob them of their headspace. People with long-term problem debts are no longer able to think about anything else other than their debts. It is good to point out that *vroegsignalering* can really add to that stress burden.

The annual amount spent in the Netherlands on helping people resolve their debts is currently EUR 17 billion, whereas the total amount of debts is only about EUR 3.5 billion per year. Arnhem's city council noticed that. The obvious conclusion is that it is much cheaper to pay the debts of the poorest to help them become unstuck.

It is a two-year experiment that includes the option of "extensive counseling" to tackle related problems such as depression, social isolation and malnutrition caused by the financial challenges.

Many households in the Netherlands with problem debts owe as much as EUR 40,000. The largest debt amount found for the households in this experiment in Arnhem is EUR 18,000. Families with children will be given priority. The maximum amount to be spent on eradicating these people's debts is EUR 700,000. Part of that also comes from for example utility companies canceling the debt.

This could be an example of what good can be done with *vroegsignalering* as it can help cities identify households that it might really be able to help this way. Hounding debtors and admonishing them as if they are 5-year-olds accomplishes nothing positive, by contrast, but just stresses people out even more and erodes confidence in government even further.

In some Dutch municipalities, the local government buys all the debts so that the municipality becomes the sole creditor. The long-term goal appears to be to lower the debtors' stress levels, thereby increasing their health and enabling them to support themselves better again.

What local governments have to acknowledge is that most debts are a simple subtraction of a greater amount from a smaller amount. More money needs to go out than is coming in.

More and more Dutch higher-income households are getting into financial difficulty. This is not because they are learning-disabled or are struggling with mental health issues or alcohol. It's because their expenses have gone up more than their incomings. They often do not apply for the tax benefits ("toeslagen") that they may be entitled to. This is not because they do not know how to fill out the forms or because they are ashamed. It's because these tax benefits are a major source of debts as they often need to be paid back again later.

Importantly, the echo of the child care tax credit scandal ("toeslagenschandaal") – for which reparations have not completed yet and in some cases can never make up for the immense damage that was done – is still reverberating around the world. Between 2005 and 2019, approximately 26,000 parents were accused of major fraud, with very severe consequences for their lives. This failure of government was so impactful that many people understandably consider the risk associated with all *toeslagen* (Dutch tax credits) unacceptably high, for which they are admonished by the *vroegsignalering* people. Can you blame people for trying to avoid such horrors? The algorithm responsible for that childcare tax credits disaster also assigned a greater fraud risk to low-income households.

It may be too well known that very little has been done to avoid a repeat. In any case, this scandal did nothing for people's trust in government and democracy. What's more, on 31 August 2024, Dutch newspaper Trouw published an article about a Dutch court case in Amsterdam involving a woman who took out a bank loan of 25,000 euro to be able to deal with the effects of that badly biased algorithm that incorrectly accused people of major fraud and ruined many people's lives.

The judge in the case warned that a repeat of this drama is actually likely. The case itself too is an example of how regulations that on the face of it are designed to help people don't. She did not qualify for help in June 2021 yet because her situation was not yet dramatic enough in June. Shortly after, in August, the bank did step up its attempts and her situation escalated, but by then she no longer qualified for help because she should have applied sooner, which she had done.

Also interesting within this context is that Princess Laurentien who's been pushing hard for justice in the matter of the algorithm disaster was criticized so harshly by civil servants in the course of 2024 that she felt that it was better for her to withdraw. (She married into the Dutch Royal family.)

The lack of information associated with *vroegsignalering* – which can be carried out by the local government's tax collection department staff – will make some people worry about whether they will end up on a list with an asterisk next to their name.

On 26 April 2024, the province of Limburg (that is, Provinciale Staten; Jasper Kuntzelaers is in charge of mobility) decided to do something about that simple extraction by offering people on a low income free public transport on a major transit company's trains and buses (Arriva's) during non-peak hours. (First, municipalities have to identify and approach these people. How this will be done is not clear to me, but this too could be where *vroegsignalering* might be able to assist.)

This initiative can be a game-changer for many, for example, because it can help people break out of the social isolation that poverty can cause. It can also mean that less money has to go out, depending on circumstances; then you're doing something about the outcome of that subtraction. But why only help people during non-peak hours?

The issue I have with these local initiatives is that they disadvantage others. Why does it have to matter that you live 10 meters beyond a province's borders yet in the same country? Why should it make a difference whether you are dirt-poor in Arnhem or in Nijmegen? (Then again, people on both sides of borders with adjacent countries could say similar things.) What does the law state? "Discriminatie wegens godsdienst, levensovertuiging, politieke gezindheid, ras, geslacht **of op welke grond dan ook**, is niet toegestaan." Tricky...

What we need is governments that not only have the guts to make daring and innovative changes, but who also coordinate these developments between countries. At the moment, the situation is such that people on low incomes largely are forced to devote their time and lives toward putting more money in the pockets of people who own housing, factories and other assets. They have little agency. As long as they receive less income than they need to support themselves, they will increasingly get into debt. They can't make ends meet and it is impossible for them to change their situation, but that too depends on the country. I can dream...

Some people decide to break out of this stranglehold by living in a vehicle, which enables them to save up, sometimes enough to be able to purchase a home next. In the Netherlands, it is against the law to spend the night in a vehicle unless it is parked at an official campsite. In many countries, it is against the law to live in harmony with nature. Even if you own land that has a cave on it, it is usually against the law to live in that cave, regardless of how well kitted out it is and how low the impact on the surroundings is. Such mechanisms force people to keep putting money in the pockets of others and leave them with little leeway.

In the UK, there has been a televised experiment – called The Big Benefits Handout or The Great British Benefits Handout – in which families on benefits were given the full maximum benefits amount for a year as a lump sum. This was £26,000 at the time, which was around 2016. I was amazed to see the results. Even one guy's business about which I had been very doubtful from the start did well.

One family apparently used less than half of the money to set up a business that they dissolved within two years, but they didn't go back on benefits. They later said that the benefits handout had changed their lives 1,000 per cent. This was also because the broadcast made them popular, particularly because of the man's chatty conversation style. Unfortunately, he passed away shortly after.

The only person who didn't get out of poverty as far as I know was a woman who desperately kept applying for jobs and used the money to make herself look more presentable, among other things. Prolonger poverty affects what you look like.

In Denver, Colorado, 800 people without housing received up to $12,000 between July 2023 and July 2024, with no obligations attached. The Denver Basic Income Project has spent over 9.8 million dollars so far. While that may sound like a lot of money, it actually saved the city half a million. The founder and executive director is entrepreneur and philanthropist Mark Donovan. The project is headed by the University of Denver's Center for Housing and Homelessness Research. It's helping people support themselves financially and really makes a difference.

Prolonged poverty can cause you to look cheap and really dopey or even ill. It's partly the result of stress and improper nutrition, but it's not the full story. Prolonged poverty really shrinks your world. You lose sight of options that may be available to you, such as technologies that you can't afford.

Your brain moves such things to the background; life is less frustrating that way so it helps lower your stress levels. It is a much more efficient way of one's brain capacity, just like when you move to a different country, your mother tongue will eventually get rusty. It doesn't mean that there is anything wrong with your cognitive abilities. It's just how the brain works. Prolonged stress doesn't help. Blame it on cortisol.

It's so sad to see consecutive UK governments to continue to regard supporting their citizens as a punitive process instead of as an empowering one. To a degree, that may be because it's become an industry. The less efficiently these programs are run, the more money ends up going to the corporations that administer part of these programs.

In the US, the stimulus checks issued by the government to help them through the Covid pandemic enabled many people to lift themselves out of poverty. While most people used it for household expenses, 15.7 per cent used the money to pay off debt and 14.1 per cent intended to apply most of it toward savings. There also was a huge surge in new microbusinesses, some of which went on to become hugely successful.

In the UK, many people were supported adequately but some who had just started a business or a new job fell into poverty because they received no support at all. In the Netherlands, support for small businesses including the self-employed may have been comparable to that in the UK. In the UK, no minimum income level was taken into account, whereas the Netherlands guaranteed financial support from at least the minimum benefits level. In the Netherlands, however, it also later led to a large debt burden when some of the received business support had to be paid back. I haven't read or heard anything about Covid support in the UK or the Netherlands having enabled people to lift themselves out of poverty. I'd welcome getting your feedback as well as seeing more research into this.

Interestingly, I find myself forced to keep adding to this chapter. On 24 May 2024, a Dutch news article announced that 600 families on benefits will be receiving EUR 150 a month extra, in a two-year experiment. These families are mostly single-parent households and they're in Amsterdam, Zaanstad and Tilburg. The rigidity of the Dutch becomes evident when you then read that the amount of EUR 150 was chosen because it is the maximum amount that these households can receive freely without losing (part of) their benefits. Municipal regulations had to be adapted to make even this small change possible.

On 16 May 2025, I read that 300 families in Amsterdam received EUR 150 the day before, as part of the abovementioned two-year trial. According to a press release, they are part of a city-run pilot to study the effects of direct financial support on poverty, stress and well-being. The project is called *"Gewoon geld geven"* ("Simply Give Money"). "The households were selected randomly, are all on welfare benefits and include at least one child under 18. The households are free to spend the money in any way they see fit. After the two-year period, however, the monthly gift will be stepped down to zero in the course of six months.

In other countries, similar experiments have sometimes resulted in people more actively looking for fulltime jobs and children doing better in school as well as in health improvements. The outcomes differ, however, and the researchers – led by Mirre Stallen – consider the Dutch situation unique relative to that in other countries.

In the same article, one expert comments that there research in the area of poverty and debt in the Netherlands is scarce. Many projects are proudly made public and are then never heard about again, she says. That same expert – Nadja Jungmann – is part of a commission that has recently has established that low income families in the Netherlands need up to several hundred euros per month more to make ends meet. However, for single-parent households, this is not the case; their level of income does meet their requirements.

5. Tips for citizens and municipalities

When I first wrote this chapter, I was still unaware of the despicable tactics that not just creditors but also municipalities apply. Maybe this shouldn't have taken me by surprise in view of the fact that the Dutch government, at all levels, is the biggest creditor and that the same departments that are tasked with offering *vroegsignalering* also serve as collection agencies.

Another factor that I am still assimilating is that the country underwent a major shift to the right during the nearly two decades that I had been away from the Netherlands. The country is far more polarized than it used to be. When I was a student here, with no financial or advisory family support, I became acutely aware of how socioeconomic inequality can affect your situation and how little the well-to-do know about this, but I never encountered contempt because I was relatively poor. That's changed dramatically, but it's complicated by the fact that I am over 55 now. That too attracts a lot of contempt.

Here's what you need to know:

Pretty early on, I'd already informed the staff at the municipality exactly what it was that I needed to resolve my situation. I'd even included different options. It was all ignored.

One of those options boiled down to basic monthly benefits (social security payments). When I later asked why they didn't even ask whether I had applied for them or suggested that I might be eligible for them, they said that this wasn't their department. Similarly, they never asked whether I had applied to have my municipal taxes waived. In practice, *vroegsignalering* appears to be little more than merely an early debt collection service that has the power of the government behind it. That needs to change.

I remember having been late with my rent in the past, when I was self-employed in Amsterdam. I received a letter about it and I called hurriedly to reassure them that there wasn't a problem. One of my biggest clients paid well, but always paid late because their internal processes were rigid and sluggish. Whenever I was busy working with them, I wouldn't take on a lot of other work. Being late with my rent once or twice wasn't a problem. If needed, we would simply talk about something like this in those days, with mutual human respect and understanding. It didn't elicit contempt or belittlement.

That seems to have changed dramatically.

I learned about *vroegsignalering* the hard way. Nobody knows that it exists and none of the people who do know about it tell you that it exists. That appears to be because they either see you as the adversary who must be conquered and tamed or the enemy that must be gotten rid of. They don't see you as an equal or as a negotiating party.

Handling your money well can include deliberately paying one bill late, so that you can pay another invoice timely. You do this because you are on top of your incomings and outgoings, but simply aren't wealthy enough or don't have enough income to pay all your bills on time all the time. You don't know that if you do that these days, you may get pestered by people from the municipality, but it all depends on which municipality you live in. The government obliges municipalities to carry out the legislation, but it has not told them how to do it. Some do almost nothing, whereas others act pretty aggressively.

Let me share some of my own experiences.

Again, I had just arrived in the country after many years abroad. I had been stuck in an abusive situation with coercive control. I'd asked for help repeatedly, but got none. I left everything behind and only had the clothes on my back and a few in my suitcases (as well as a tent). My monthly income in the Netherlands where I no longer really knew anyone well – isolation is a frequent side effect of abuse situations – was only around 500 euro. Part of my *vroegsignalering* problem may have been that people simply refused to believe that I had that little income. I don't know. I can only guess.

The last thing I needed was more abuse and coercive control. I was very eager to get my life back on its feet, of course. The first thing that this required was replacing my phones as they'd all gotten hacked abroad. That required money.

Unfortunately, most people still think as if we are all still using mechanical typewriters and fountain pens. They can't wrap their brains around the reality of the digital world. This is also the issue behind the Post Office scandal in the UK and the childcare tax credits scandal in the Netherlands.

Because of my age and because I'm a woman, these folks tend to assume that I can't handle technology. Among other things, I learned some programming as part of my Master's, have built computers from scratch and created huge websites as html in NotePad. I was using Macs and Windows computers and programmed a modem so that I could do email with it when these local *vroegsignalering* people hadn't even been born yet. They are the newbies, but if you're a woman of over 55 or 45 and mention hacking, nobody is willing to listen to you except people with the same or a better knowledge of IT. I've stopped mentioning hacking altogether. I no longer bother trying to explain.

I've also stopped mentioning my now very different cultural background. Dutch people don't want to know why I behave differently. I've also learned that if people are biased about who you are and what you are like, they tend to experience you as unpleasant and disagreeable if you don't confirm that they are right about what they think you are and what you should behave like.

Because of income that I had still had abroad, I didn't instantly qualify for Dutch "bijstand" benefits (social security) and it's useless to apply early. (If you receive this lowest level of benefits, you are not allowed to earn a penny these days. You need to report it all and it all comes out of your next benefit payment. So it can really keep you stuck.)

The application process can take two months, though. It can take longer if you are highly educated but penniless. They may for example suspect that you sold your business and are hiding the proceeds, so they'd investigate that first. So it seemed to me that it was much better to focus on generating my own income again as soon as possible. However, I had not counted on *vroegsignalering* and everything it can result in wanting to take over my life. It was a bit like someone throwing a stick into the spokes of a bicycle wheel.

Eventually, things started happening that were very worrisome and really scared me. I suspect that this was done because people were eager to find an excuse that would allow them to get rid of me or grab control of all aspects of my life. At this point, I had never spoken with any of these people, not even over the phone, and they never asked me any questions about anything. Someone, however, appears to have claimed that I was a threat to myself and/or people around me. That unleashed a great deal of nonsense that took over my life for a while. Nothing was put in writing, however. I asked for a letter, and one was promised but never sent. People repeatedly lied to me within *this* context, too, and played despicable games.

I've recently learned that this may have been mostly revenge for a negative Google review. I don't know who exactly started what, however. It's possible that some people who acted despicably from my point of view were simply fooled. I can only guess.

What now follows first was the impression that I had until someone recently angrily mentioned that Google review. That person represented my creditor. They had ceased all communication with me nearly 10 months earlier... Because of a Google review? That's pretty crazy if you ask me. I've meanwhile removed that Google review. That is not because I felt intimidated but because I don't want to be associated with the party in question and also because I am contemplating a different approach toward making things better at that organization.

The Netherlands is a highly prosperous country and it used to be highly egalitarian. As a result, if you pay a bill late, people who know about it tend to assume that you have plenty of income, but are spending it all on luxury goods or have a gambling addiction, that you have an intellectual disability or are developing dementia. Maybe you are hoarding and if they go into your home, they might find stacks and stacks of unopened Amazon boxes or illegal drugs.

People working for the municipality asked me repeatedly who I was associating with – which is none of their business – and they also started insisting that they needed to see inside my home. What on earth for?

Initially, *vroegsignalering* meant that I received an undated card in my mailbox one day stating that someone from the municipality had been to my door because my rent was late. The term *vroegsignalering* wasn't mentioned. The card said that if I wanted to, I could get help – no strings attached – and the examples mentioned on the card seemed to be based on the assumption that I might have dementia or was learning-disabled.

I ignored the card. I assumed that it was meant well, but I also saw it as a violation of my privacy. I don't follow them home and start knocking on the doors of strangers just because I stood next in line at the supermarket checkout and noticed that they asked the cashier to take the pizza off because they didn't have enough money. Why would some stranger do that to me? I was baffled. Whether this was genuine or a scam didn't matter to me at this point.

The approach taken by the municipality, however, is the same one as many scammers have adopted. We are all warned to ignore strangers who knock on our doors out of the blue or who contact us "to offer help". It is hard to understand that a local municipality would operate in such an amateurish manner.

Next, I received a letter from someone else at the municipality who claimed to have been to my door as well. This letter was dated and stated that the department had no phone number or email address for me. They could have found an email address for me on the internet. More important is that I discovered that the "wrong number" call that I thought I had received was actually from that department when I received another call from that same number. Why did they feel the need to lie about not having any contact information for me?

It just so happens that a magazine for Dutch civil servants published an interview with this second person. It's freely available online and offers a inside view of the world of "vroegsignalering" and "preventie".

I initially thought of her and her colleagues as amateurish "huppelkutjes" (silly naïve people with little life experience), but it's meanwhile dawned on me that they deliberately apply manipulative and deceitful tactics that people with a narcissistic personality disorder also often use.

Their behavior may partially stem from naivety (lack of life experience), but it is dominated by bias, prejudice and even contempt. It is dictated by the parties that hold the power. In this specific situation, it's not the municipality. The biggest real estate owner in town determines what happens at the municipality.

At this particular municipality, the department that deals with debts goes by three different names and silly games are played with that alone. The employees that work there don't want to assist people. They want to control them and want to control their lives. They even practice their interactions in role play simulations. That's what I learned from the published interview.

All employees that I have met with at this municipality applied verbal manipulation. They combine aggressive or insulting statements and even vague threats with appeasing and cooperative gestures. These gestures initially come across as wonderful, certainly if they were preceded by threatening or aggressive tones. It aims to build trust. It appears to offer the reassurance that these people genuinely want to help.

However, these reassurances never show up in emails or letters and none of these wonderfully cooperative gestures are upheld in practice. They evaporate into thin air. Once you notice that, any trust you may have had will quickly disappear, particularly if you keep in mind that there also were phrases or behaviors that made you feel uncomfortable. I assume that the latter is intended to undermine your confidence so that you will be more susceptible to the reassurances, hence easier to control.

If you ask these folks to put down any of these reassurances in writing, you may find them balking and stamping their feet. They'll get angry.

Then they may try to manipulate you again. They may say something like: "But we had such a wonderful conversation last time!"

We didn't. I may have seemed chatty, but I mostly kept my thoughts to myself because I was making worrisome observations. I did not consciously pick up on the verbal manipulation attempts, but I may have noticed them nevertheless. Because of these techniques that these employees have been taught and aim to apply, the conversation tends to be a bit odd. This is confusing and may make you a little wary. The threatening tone in which one of them conveyed that she really wanted to see inside my home didn't exactly help.

More importantly, while these employees may have been taught verbal manipulation techniques, body language gave one of them away. Her movements revealed her true thoughts and intentions. I was not looking for it. I merely witnessed it.

This particular person was much too eager to tick a box that would take my agency away. Her pen kept hovering above it. She even mentioned, almost muttering to herself, that she could always still do this later. (That I might be mentally incompetent had been hinted at before.)

She also literally jumped out of her chair, however, when I talked about how I had negotiated a large settlement with the lawyers for two insurance companies in a lawsuit that I had conducted as a pro se (litigant in person), acting for myself abroad. ("See? I am quite capable.

Please, please, please believe me, pretty please. I do not have dementia. I am not learning-disabled.") If she really wanted to help, she would have been pleased to see that I was far from helpless. This person was *not* interested in helping me. This person was eager to start controlling my life. She saw me as an adversary, as a pest.

(Update: On 27 June 2025, I read in an article on the NOS website that Dutch people tend to believe that you are a bad person if you start a lawsuit against a company. I had no idea.)

According to the published interview, this person used to be employed at a collection agency, but didn't like the idea that she was working for creditors. She wanted to help people instead, she claims. Ironically, she then took up a job with the country's biggest household debt creditor. How did she find this job? Someone who used to work at the same collection agency told her about a vacancy at her new place of work, the local municipality.

In the interview, she talks about how people like me initially "resist" their "assistance" and how the employees engage in role play to learn to deal with people like me. Might that be mostly well-educated or simply somewhat intelligent people or people with a great deal of life experience, people who can tell when someone is trying to bamboozle them? She does not strike me as the type that suffers from rescuer syndrome because she happens to have a second income source that relies on pure consumerism. She is not rehabbing wildlife or working with refugees.

So what I initially advised municipalities in this chapter – most of it still follows because it is valid – was basically a load of naïve crock in the case of this particular municipality. Should I mention that I actually innocently reached out to this department, months ago, when I noticed how amateurish they seemed to be operating? I've even suggested that they start an exchange process with other municipalities so staff gets to see how the process is handled elsewhere. They can all learn from each other that way. (The municipality that I am talking about is pretty small. The staff comes across as a handful of people who all know each other.)

In my defense, I had not spoken with any of these people yet at that point and I gave them the benefit of the doubt. I had no clue what on earth I was dealing with. It all felt like a pretty bad movie.

True, most of it had felt like a massive revenge exercise or plain bullying pretty early on, notably on the part of the person who made the first contact attempt and had left the undated card. I have since spoken with her over the phone once and was appalled by her contemptuous and angry attitude. That was about half a year after she'd left the undated card. She was the one who had managed to unleash a smelly torrent of sewerage in my direction without ever having spoken with me. It seems she wanted to teach me – someone who is no longer in her twenties or someone whose income is low - my proper place in the order of things.

To be specific, she was the one who alerted mental health services (part of and paid for by the municipality) and I was swatted. She may have been pushed to do so by someone else. I don't know. I can only guess. Nothing had happened, nothing at all. The creditor may have pushed for this; the representative that I recently spoke with suggested that another, unrelated third party might be responsible for it. (No.) Why did she try to blame someone else?

Mental health services kept pestering me for a long time and even tried to gaslight me about appointments that I was supposed to have missed but that I didn't actually have. Why? It was awfully unpleasant, highly distracting and pretty despicable.

I am really appalled by this. If they feel free to do this to me, someone who is reasonably able to stand up for herself, then how do they treat health minorities such as autistic people? How do they deal with refugees? They scared me, they really scared me. And that was only for starters...

Pretty early on already, I tried to use privacy legislation to stop them from pestering me. They've refused, but they didn't merely refuse. They sent me a registered letter dated exactly two months after my own registered letter, asking me for ID, which I provided. Then they sent me another registered letter in which they stated that they refused to comply.

I'm pretty sure that I am dealing with malicious activity. Why do I say that? For starters, nobody has ever asked me about any health conditions, any medications I might take or even who provides my healthcare. Negative rumors appear to have been spread about me that some people may have taken seriously. I don't know. I can only guess. There's been a remarkable unwillingness to put anything in writing.

Also, when I asked a third party to remove my data, they complied instantly and they didn't ask for ID. That was the water board, because they seem to be expected to exchange data with not only the municipality but also whoever you rent your home from, if you rent. The second party that I asked to remove data they held for me within this context was the municipality itself. They haven't exactly complied either.

Extra confusing was that I had also been asking simple questions about my utilities that people kept refusing to answer. People were dodging and I found it really strange. I started wondering whether this might be the main reason for what was happening to me. How could I not? I made some calculations and I had to consider that I might be dealing with an organization that was committing fraud to the tune of 8 million euro per year or more. While I think that something else is going on here (a matter of balancing the books, so to speak), I can't rule out large-scale fraud either, however. Not a pleasant idea.

I have not yet been able to get my life back on its feet, but that is now also because I no longer have a desire to stay. The *vroegsignalering* upheaval also ended up delaying my application for basic *bijstand* benefits by half a year, by the way. There is not much you can do on an income of 500 euros per month, certainly not if you have to spend time, money and effort on fighting off the *vroegsignalering* circus and everything around it.

Municipalities who really want to serve their citizens will and those who don't won't. It's as simple as that.

Those who really want to help citizens with little income should select employees who deal with *vroegsignalering* wisely. Avoid the obvious choice for people with rescuer syndrome. They see problems where there are none and they will also take those problems home. Find calm unflappable people who've been around. Ensure sufficient diversity, too.

Train and support your staff regardless of how much life and employment experience they have. Don't teach them how to be manipulative but how to deal with their own biases and stress.

People who contact debtors within this *vroegsignalering* process should have personal experience with debts. As matters stand, there are many misconceptions about "the kinds of people who get into debt". A common assumption is for example that people who have debts do not know how to complete forms and therefore do not apply for certain funds or have succumbed to stress and are ignoring their bills.

The way things are it is very important that employees being tasked with *vroegsignalering* assignments from within the local municipality receive training and psychological counseling. They should receive training regarding how to approach debtors, also taking neurodiversity and cultural differences into account.

They should receive support as well. If they have never had debts themselves, they can be so freaked out over the mere notion that they transfer their own insecurity and fear to the debtors. That is not helpful in any way. If that is the case, then there is also a risk that these employees take worries home and are on their way to a burnout.

It can also be highly counterproductive when what they may experience as heartfelt concern and disappointment comes across as boredom or merely personal frustration motivated by their need to meet their employer's requirements.

- Always first contact the citizen by sending a friendly letter in which you do not talk down to the person, but describe the concept of *vroegsignalering*. Give complete, clear and transparent information. This can be concise. Use an envelope that states "this is an official communication from your local municipality". Make clear that the communication is not from a scammer and tell them that they can verify that by taking the letter to the municipality and asking to speak with whoever claims to have sent it. If the name under the letter is that of someone who works at the municipality, the letter can still be from a scammer who is pretending to be that person. The first step **has** to be independent verification.
- Explain who exactly has contacted the municipality about what supposed debt and when. State the amount and the date. Verify whether the debtor had given the creditor in question permission to contact you. Do not walk over the person's rights. Ask whether and how you might be able to help. State that you may be able to help and give examples, such as that you may be able to waive local taxes if the income is low enough and that you may also be able to help them get their water board bill waived or that you can offer payment in installments "if

that would be helpful".

- If your municipality has the option to place debtors on a no-contact list, you should give the consumer that information too. (Please do not call it a blacklist as some municipalities do.)
- Debtors should always be allowed or encouraged to retain or regain a sense of agency and control.
- People with debts are easy targets for scammers because people with debts are often very eager to clear their debts.
- If you meet with these citizens, always try to meet at city hall or a similar location. It is not only much less invasive and more respectful, but can also enable you to spend less time while achieving the same results.

Do not make a house visit or phone call your first contact attempt.

- Many people ignore phone calls from numbers that they don't recognize.
- Simply going to someone's home, unannounced and uninvited, expecting the person to be present and then instantly mentioning the person's arrears with company Y is extremely invasive and disrespectful. Would you like to have this happen to you?
- Banks and others warn their clients not to trust anyone who turns up on their doorstep unannounced.
- Unannounced visits can also cause upset for some autistic people and if it concerns a family, the woman may be breastfeeding or bathing a baby when you ring the doorbell.
- Do your best not to skirt the law and avoid being evasive. Give clear, honest answers. How will you ever be able to get respect and honesty from the other party if you are not willing to offer it first?
- Remain aware of biases. This is why training is important. It's not true that all people with foreign names are scamming the system, just like it is not true that everyone over 55 has Alzheimer's, for example. Also be aware of the power imbalance and do your best not to abuse it. This aspect too should be part of staff training.
- Staff engaging in *vroegsignalering* shouldn't even assume that the people who they want to approach are locals who have lived locally all their lives and for example refer to local venues and

parties as if the debtor undoubtedly is familiar with them. They shouldn't assume either that the debtors undoubtedly will have very little education.

- Some of the people they approach may be autistic. Others may be deaf or blind or have fled from persecution or have lost everything in a nasty divorce. Staff should know how to take all of this into account and tread lightly. All of this should be part of training and support for these employees.

Again, it should of course not be staff at the largest household debt creditor that is asked to assist debtors and mediate in the first place. It should be a specialized neutral party, with no financial interests. This would require independent funding for that party and this funding should very simply be based on the number of inhabitants in a municipality, nothing else.

It should not be based on demographics as middle-class people have debts too and those who are accustomed to making do with little money are often much more experienced. It should be possible, however, for such debt assistance agencies to shift funds to one another at different locations if the need arises.

I cannot stress the following enough. Do not assume that debts are the results of behavioral problems or intellectual deficits. With inequality and right-wing tendencies increasing in the Netherlands, debts are now far more often simply the result of a subtraction of a larger number from a previous smaller number, the latter number being people's income. As the *Nationale Ombudsman* stated repeatedly in his report, the minimum level of income in the Netherlands no longer suffices to keep expenses manageable.

6. Credit references

To my knowledge, the Netherlands does not have credit score agencies such as for example in the United Kingdom, but it does have a national credit reference agency called the BKR. In 2023 and 2024, my record in this system was clean.

In April 2025, when I decided to check again, I discovered that the BKR now has a separate website where individual citizens can check their credit record (loans etc). The main website now has a section "*Vroegsignalering*" to which citizens have no access. That is very worrisome.

Vroegsignaleringsregister (Vindplaats van Schulden VPS)

In het vroegsignaleringsregister verzamelen we via ons platform Vindplaats van Schulden (VPS) signalen over mensen met betalingsachterstanden bij vaste lasten partners, zoals zorgverzekeraars, verhuurders van woningen en nutsbedrijven.

Bent u een vaste lasten partner? Dan heeft u een belangrijke rol bij het voorkomen van problematische schulden bij uw klanten. Heeft uw klant een betalingsachterstand, dan dient u eerst zelf de openstaande vordering te innen (sociaal verantwoord incasso). Pas als u zich heeft ingespannen om de vordering voldaan te krijgen, bent u verplicht dit signaal via het platform Vindplaats van Schulden in een vroeg stadium aan uw gemeente door te geven.

Werkt u bij een gemeente? Dan bent u er dankzij de signalen in VPS tijdig bij als inwoners een betalingsachterstand krijgen.

References

Banijay Documentaries (2019). The Great British Benefits Handout. https://www.youtube.com/playlist?list=PLyRqK5BQ11x1vRyM-94xpPwVL1ZTdobAP Also available on Amazon Prime and elsewhere.

Bergthaler, Wolfgang, Garrido, Jose, and Rosha, Anjum (2023) The Right Tool for the Job? Mortgage Distress and Personal Insolvency during the European Debt Crisis. IMF Working Paper 92, WP/23/92. https://www.imf.org/-/media/Files/Publications/WP/2023/English/wpiea2023092-print-pdf.ashx

Bregman, Rutger (2017) Poverty isn't a lack of character; it's a lack of cash. TED Talk. https://www.youtube.com/watch?v=ydKcaIE6O1k

Denver Basic Income Project https://www.denverbasicincomeproject.org/

Farrer, Martin (2019) Historian berates billionaires at Davos over tax avoidance. The Guardian. https://www.theguardian.com/business/2019/jan/30/historian-berates-billionaires-at-davos-over-tax-avoidance

Nationale Ombudsman (2024) Hoe eerder hoe beter. Rapportnummer 2024/005.
https://www.nationaleombudsman.nl/publicaties/onderzoeken/hoe-eerder-hoe-beter

NOS Nieuws (2024) Proef om gegevens over beginnende schulden eerder te delen met gemeenten. https://nos.nl/artikel/2537920-proef-om-gegevens-over-beginnende-schulden-eerder-te-delen-met-gemeenten

Reifner, U. et al., 2003, Consumer Overindebtedness and Consumer Law in the European Union: Final Report (report presented to the Comm. of the European Communities, Health and Consumer Protec. Directorate-General, Sept. 2003)
http://www.knl.lv/raksti_data/1147/parskats_ES_2003.pdf

Stacey, Kiran (2024) Labour moves to end no-fault evictions within months.
https://www.theguardian.com/money/article/2024/sep/06/labour-moves-to-end-no-fault-evictions-within-months

Stewart, Rory (2024) To end extreme poverty, give cash — not advice. TED Talk.
https://www.ted.com/talks/rory_stewart_to_end_extreme_poverty_give_cash_not_advice
See also https://www.rorystewart.co.uk/

United Nations (2022) Like racism and sexism, 'povertyism' should be illegal, UN rights expert says.
https://news.un.org/en/story/2022/11/1130267

Wet gemeentelijke schuldhulpverlening
https://wetten.overheid.nl/BWBR0031331/

About the author

Angelina Souren's primary background is in the earth & life sciences, but she has now spent over a decade looking at issues that are all part of the field of bioethics. That includes inequality.

Although she went to university relatively late in life, she graduated cum laude from VU University Amsterdam. Prior to her scientific endeavors, she used to work in the tourism and hospitality sector in Amsterdam, interacting with people from many different cultural backgrounds.

She spent most of her adult life in the Netherlands in and around Amsterdam, but she didn't grow up there. She's emigrated several times and is very familiar with England and also with Florida. As part of her Master's, she carried out geological fieldwork in Sweden and Spain.

She's worked at and with researchers and other staff at various universities and other organizations, in employment as well as in self-employment.

Among other things, she is a former board member of the Environmental Chemistry (and Toxicology) Section at the Royal Netherlands Chemical Society. She served as associate editor for the U.S.-based Geochemical Society for over a decade.

Health-wise, she's blessed. She has an IQ of 133 and dementia does not run in her family. Cancer certainly does, but this concerns different types of cancer so even that is not a factor of concern. She has a minor spinal deformity that runs in her mother's family and so does musical talent.

Her mother succumbed to vastly metastasized breast cancer a long time ago, her father to lung cancer much later in life. Both her parents had little more than primary school. Her mother was a home-maker. Her dad was self-employed for a long time and provided very well for his family.

If you want to connect with her, you can try emailing her at angelinasouren@gmail.com.

Thanks for having purchased this booklet.